The **Golden** Retriever

Buying, nutrition, care, behavior, health, reproduction and lots more

Contents

Foreword

The book you are holding is not intended to be a complete "owner's manual" for the Golden Retriever. If we had tried to cover all the information available about this breed, its history and development, feeding, training, health, ailments and whatever more, this would be a book of at least 500 pages.

What we have done however, is to collect basic information to help the (future) owner of a Golden Retriever look after his or her pet responsibly. Too many people still buy a pet before really understanding what they're about to get into.

This book goes into the broad history of the Golden Retriever, the breed standard and some pros and cons of buying a Golden. You will also find essential information on feeding, initial training and an introduction into reproduction. Finally we give attention to daily care, health and some breed-specific ailments.

Based on this information, you can buy a Golden Retriever, having thought it through carefully, and keep it as a pet in a responsible manner. Our advice, though, is not just to leave it to this small book. A properly brought-up and well-trained dog is more than just a dog. Invest a little extra in a puppy training course or an obedience course. There are also excellent books available that go deeper into certain aspects than is possible here.

The *About Pets* editorial team

ibooks

Distributed by Simon & Schuster

Distributed by Simon & Schuster, Inc.
1230 Avenue of the Americas,
New York, NY 10020

ibooks, inc.
24 West 25th Street
New York, NY 10010
ISBN 0-7434-4525-2
First ibooks, inc. printing
October 2002
10 9 8 7 6 5 4 3 2 1

Senior Consultant Lisa K. Allen, DVM
Cover photograph

Cover design by j. vita

As the purchaser of this book, you are entitled to access a free electronic book version of the title for use with Windows, Macintosh and Palm computers and PDAs. To access the "ebook" version, you may log onto www.ibooks.net, click the "About Pets" button and follow the directions.

Original title: *De golden retriever*

Photos:
Rob Dekker, WMP, Freddy Quackelbeen,
Charles Borgmans, fam. Kuipers,
H. Broekhuizen, M. Groeneveld,
Y. Coot, J. M. Kosse, E. Berkhout,
H. Vliem en Jos Stouthuyzen
Printed in China

In General

The Golden Retriever owes its wide popularity to its friendly appearance and affectionate character.

Although most Goldens these days are kept as house pets, their talent for hunting remains unmistakable. Moreover, the Golden Retriever possesses a strong will to please: it enjoys carrying out some task or other for its master. This will to please means that you can take part in various activities with a Golden (you can read more about that later in this book).

Family members

The Golden Retriever is one of six retriever breeds. To retrieve, of course, means to bring something back, and comes from the hunting world. Retrievers are dogs that come into their own after the shot. The hunter shoots his quarry and the dog's job is to bring it to him. Because the targets are often waterfowl (that are shot in the air above the water), retrievers also need to be excellent swimmers. Besides the Golden, the best known retriever is the Labrador. The other members of the retriever family are the Flat-Coated Retriever, the Curly-Coated Retriever, the Chesapeake Bay Retriever and the Nova Scotia Duck Tolling Retriever.

Character

Every dog is an individual. But Golden Retrievers also have a breed-specific character, which has to do with their original use as a hunting dog. The most important character trait of a Golden Retriever is its will to please. It's a working dog that loves to work off its energy. If it doesn't get enough attention and exercise, it will try to work off its energy in the home and will become a restless, nervous dog. A Golden Retriever that is allowed to use its enthusiasm in the right way is friendly and happy. It can guard, but will normally greet visitors with a wagging tail. It will also get on well with other dogs. A Golden's favorite pastimes are tracking and retrieving. It has an excellent sense of smell and loves to use it. It remains playful up to an advanced age, and will zealously bring back anything you throw. And if you throw a ball or a stick into water you'll make its day. A Golden Retriever is one of the best swimmers among dogs, and they will seldom walk past a stream or pond without taking a dip!

Origins

The Golden Retriever has its origins in Scotland, where different dogs were used for each type of hunt: terriers were used to hunt small wild animals; bloodhounds were used for bigger game.

Following the development of more and more accurate hunting guns, hunters now needed dogs that could retrieve their kill over longer distances. This type of hunting did not need an aggressive dog, but one that would calmly wait at its post until needed; it needed a good nose, good swimming ability (and could stand cold water) and the ability to retrieve the kill undamaged. The yellow Flat- or Wavy-Coated Retriever, Nous, is regarded as the ancestor of the breed. Lord Tweedmouth crossed this male with the Tweed Water Spaniel bitch Belle in 1868. This breed (now extinct) was an excellent retrieving dog. The puppies of Nous and Belle were bred again, and a Red Setter was also crossed in. For the first few years the dogs from this line were still registered as Flat- or Wavy- Coated Retrievers. In 1913, a separate register was opened—that of the "Retriever (Golden or Yellow)." The British Golden Retriever Club was founded in 1911, and in 1920, the name "Golden Retriever" was officially recognized.

Breed standard

A standard has been developed for all breeds recognized by the American Kennel Club (reprinted on the following pages). This standard provides a guideline for breeders and inspectors. It is something of an ideal that dogs of the breed must strive to match. With some breeds, dogs are already bred that match the ideal. Other breeds have a long way to go.

There is a list of defects for each breed. These can be serious defects that disqualify the dog, and it will be excluded from breeding. Permitted defects are

not serious, but do cost points in a show.

The AKC breed standard for the Golden Retriever

General Appearance

A symmetrical, powerful, active dog, sound and well put together, not clumsy nor long in the leg, displaying a kindly expression and possessing a personality that is eager, alert and self-confident. Primarily a hunting dog, he should be shown in hard-working condition. Overall appearance, balance, gait and purpose to be given more emphasis than any of his component parts.

Faults

Any departure from the described ideal shall be considered faulty to the degree to which it interferes with the breed's purpose or is contrary to breed character.

Size, Proportion, Substance

Males 23–24 inches in height at withers; females 21 1/2–22 1/2 inches. Dogs up to one inch above or below standard size should be proportionately penalized. Deviation in height of more than one inch from the standard shall disqualify. Length from breastbone to point of buttocks slightly greater than height at withers in ratio of 12:11. Weight for dogs 65–75 pounds; bitches 55–65 pounds.

Head

Broad in skull, slightly arched laterally and longitudinally without prominence of frontal bones

(forehead) or occipital bones. Stop well defined but not abrupt. Foreface deep and wide, nearly as long as skull. Muzzle straight in profile, blending smoothly and strongly into skull; when viewed in profile or from above, slightly deeper and wider at stop than at tip. No heaviness in flews. Removal of whiskers is permitted but not preferred.

Eyes
Friendly and intelligent in expression, medium large with dark, close-fitting rims, set well apart and reasonably deep in sockets. Color preferably dark brown; medium brown acceptable. Slant eyes and narrow, triangular eyes detract from correct expression and are to be faulted. No white or haw visible when looking straight ahead. Dogs showing evidence of functional abnormality of eyelids or eyelashes (such as, but not limited to, trichiasis, entropion, ectropion, or distichiasis) are to be excused from the ring.

Ears
Rather short with front edge attached well behind and just above the eye and falling close to cheek. When pulled forward, tip of ear should just cover the eye. Low, hound-like ear set to be faulted.

Nose
Black or brownish black, though fading to a lighter shade in cold weather not serious. Pink nose or one seriously lacking in pigmentation to be faulted.

Teeth
Scissors bite, in which the outer side of the lower incisors touches the inner side of the upper incisors. Undershot or overshot bite is a disqualification. Misalignment of teeth (irregular placement of incisors) or a level bite (incisors, meet each other edge to edge) is undesirable, but not to be confused with undershot or overshot. Full dentition, obvious gaps are serious faults.

Neck, Topline, Body
Neck medium long, merging gradually into well-laid back shoulders, giving sturdy, muscular appearance. Untrimmed natural ruff. No throatiness.

Back line strong and level from withers to slightly sloping croup, whether standing or moving. Sloping back line, roach or sway back, flat or steep croup to be faulted.

Body well-balanced, short coupled, deep through the chest. Chest between forelegs at least as wide as a man's closed hand including thumb, with well developed forechest. Brisket extends to elbow. Ribs long and well sprung but not barrel shaped, extending well towards hindquarters. Loin short, muscular, wide and deep, with very little tuck-up.

Slabsidedness, narrow chest, lack of depth in brisket, excessive tuck-up, flat or steep croup to be faulted.

Tail

Well set on, thick and muscular at the base, following the natural line of the croup. Tail bones extend to, but not below, the point of hock. Carried with merry action, level or with some moderate upward curve; never curled over back nor between legs.

Forequarters

Muscular, well coordinated with hindquarters and capable of free movement. Shoulder blades long and well laid back with upper tips fairly close together at withers. Upper arms appear about the same length as the blades, setting the elbows back beneath the upper tip of the blades, close to the ribs without looseness. Legs, viewed from the front, straight with good bone, but not to the point of coarseness. Pasterns short and strong, sloping slightly with no suggestion of weakness. Dew claws on forelegs may be removed, but are normally left on.

Feet

Medium size, round, compact and well knuckled, with thick pads. Excess hair may be trimmed to show natural size and contour. Splayed or hare feet to be faulted.

Hindquarters

Broad and strongly muscled. Profile of croup slopes slightly; the pelvic bone slopes at a slightly greater angle (approximately 30 degrees from horizontal). In a natural stance, the femur joins the pelvis at approximately a 90 degree angle; stifles well bent; hocks well let down with short, strong rear pasterns. Legs straight when viewed from rear. Cow hocks, spread hocks, and sickle hocks to be faulted.

Coat

Dense and water repellent with good undercoat. Outer coat firm and resilient, neither coarse nor silky, lying close to body; may be straight or wavy. Untrimmed natural ruff; moderate feathering on back of forelegs and on underbody; heavier feathering on front of neck, back of thighs and underside of tail. Coat on head, paws and front of legs is short and even. Excessive length, open coats and limp, soft coats are very undesirable. Feet may be trimmed and stray hairs neatened, but the natural appearance of coat or outline should not be altered by cutting or clipping.

Color

Rich, lustrous golden of various shades. Feathering may be lighter than rest of coat. With the exception of graying or whitening of face or body due to age, any white marking, other than a few white hairs on the chest, should be penalized according to its extent. Allowable light shadings are not to be confused with white markings. Predominant body color which is either extremely pale or extremely dark is undesirable. Some latitude should be given to the light puppy whose coloring shows promise of deepening with maturity. Any noticeable area of black or other off-color hair is a serious fault.

Gait

When trotting, gait is free, smooth, powerful and well coordinated, showing good reach. Viewed from any position, legs turn neither in nor out, nor do feet cross or interfere with each other. As speed increases, feet tend to converge toward center line of balance. It is recommended that dogs be shown on a loose lead to reflect true gait.

Temperament

Friendly, reliable and trustworthy. Quarrelsomeness or hostility towards other dogs or people in normal situations, or an unwarranted show of timidity or nervousness, is not in keeping with Golden Retriever character. Such actions should be penalized according to their significance.

Disqualifications

1. Deviation in height of more than one inch from standard either way.
2. Undershot or overshot bite.

Breed standard courtesy of the American Kennel Club.

Buying a Golden Retriever

Once you've made that properly considered decision to buy a dog, there are several options. Should it be a puppy, an adult dog, or even an older dog?

Should it be a bitch or dog, a pedigree dog or a mixed breed? Of course, the question also comes up as to where to buy your dog from a private person, a reliable breeder or an animal shelter? For you and the animal, it's vital to get these questions sorted out in advance. You want a dog that will fit your circumstances properly. With a puppy, you get a playful energetic housemate that will easily adapt to a new environment. If you want something quieter, an older dog is a good choice.

Pros and cons of the Golden Retriever

A Golden Retriever is an affectionate family dog that is friendly towards children and has a pleasant nature. But it's also a dog that needs a rigorous upbringing. A poorly-trained Golden is likely to be an over-enthusiastic runner that has difficulty understanding the command, "Come!"

Golden Retrievers need an above-average amount of exercise. Because they're real water rats, they will regularly get soaked. And if you're looking for an alert guard dog, you're looking at the wrong breed.

Male or female?

Whether you choose a male or a female puppy, or an adult dog or bitch, is an entirely personal decision. A male typically needs more leadership because he tends to be more dominant in nature. He will try to play boss over other dogs and, if he gets the chance, over people too. In the wild, the most dominant dog (or wolf) is always the leader of the pack. In many cases this is a male. A bitch is much more focused on her master; she sees him as the pack leader.

A puppy test is good for defining what kind of character a young dog will develop. During a test one usually sees that a dog is more dominant than a bitch. You can often quickly recognize the bossy, the adventurous and the cautious characters. So visit the litter a couple of times early on. Try to pick a puppy that suits your own personality. A dominant dog, for instance, needs a strong hand. It will often try to see how far it can go. You must regularly make it clear who's the boss and that it must obey all the members of the family.

When bitches are sexually mature, they will go into season. On average, a bitch is in season twice a year for about two or three weeks. This is the fertile period when she can become pregnant. Particularly in the second half of her season, she will want to go looking for a dog to mate with. A male dog will show more masculine traits once he is sexually mature. He will make sure other dogs know what territory is his by urinating as often as possible in as many places as he can. He is also difficult to restrain if there's a bitch in season nearby. As far as normal care is concerned there is little difference between a dog and a bitch.

Puppy or adult?

After you've made the decision for a male or female, the next question comes up. Should it be a puppy or an adult dog? Your household circumstances usually play a major role here.

Of course, it's great having a sweet little puppy in your home, but bringing up a young dog costs a lot of time. In the first year of its life it learns more than during the rest of its life. This is the period when the foundations are laid for elementary matters such as house-training, obedience and social behavior. You must reckon with the fact that your puppy will keep you busy for a couple of hours a day, certainly in the first few months. You won't need so much time with a grown dog. It has already been brought up, but this doesn't mean it doesn't need correcting from time to time.

A puppy will no doubt leave a trail of destruction in its wake for the first few months. With a little bad luck, this will cost you a number of rolls of wallpaper, some good shoes and a few socks. In the worst case you'll be left with some chewed furniture. Some puppies even manage to tear curtains from their rails. With good upbringing this

"vandalism" will quickly disappear, but you may not have to worry about this if you get an older dog. The greatest advantage of a puppy, of course, is that you can bring it up your own way. And the upbringing a dog gets (or doesn't get) is a major influence on its whole character. Finally, financial aspects may play a role in your choice. A puppy is generally (much) more expensive than an adult dog, not only in purchase price but also in "maintenance." A puppy needs to go to the veterinarian more often for the necessary vaccinations and check-ups.

Overall, bringing up a puppy costs a good deal of energy, time and money, but you have its upbringing in your own hands. An adult dog costs less money and time, but its character is already formed. You should also try to find out about the background of an adult dog. Its previous owner may have formed its character in somewhat less positive ways.

Two dogs?

Having two or more dogs in the house is not just nice for us, but also for the animals themselves. Dogs get a lot of pleasure from their own company. After all, they are pack animals.

If you're sure that you want two young dogs, it's best not to buy them at the same time. Raising a dog and establishing the bond between dog and master takes

time, and you need to give a lot of attention to your dog in this phase. Having two puppies in the house means you have to divide your attention between them. Apart from that, there's a danger that they will focus on one another rather than on their master. Buy the second pup when the first is (almost) an adult.

Two adult dogs can happily be brought into the home together, as long as they're used to each other. If this is not the case, then they have to go through that process. This is usually best achieved by letting them get to know each other on neutral territory. This prevents fights for territory. On neutral territory, perhaps an acquaintance's backyard where neither dog has been before, both dogs are basically equal. Once they've gotten to know each other, you can take them both home, and they can sort out the hierarchy there amongst themselves. In any event, don't get involved in trying to "arbitrate." That is human nature, but for the dog that's at the top of the pecking order it's like having its position undone. It will only make the dog more dominant in behavior, with all the consequences. Once the hierarchy is established, most dogs can get along fine together.

Getting a puppy when the first dog is somewhat older often has a positive effect on the older dog. The influence of the puppy almost seems to give it a second childhood. The older dog, if it's been well brought up, can help with the up-bringing of the puppy. Young dogs like to imitate the behavior of their elders. Don't forget to give both dogs the same amount of attention. Take both out alone at least once per day during the first eighteen months. Give the older dog enough opportunity to get some peace and quiet. It won't want an enthusiastic youngster running around under its feet all the time. Moreover, a puppy needs plenty of sleep and may have to have the brakes put on it once in a while.

The combination of a male and female needs special attention, and it's good advice to get a second dog of the same sex. This will avoid a lot of problems. Steril-ization and castration—spaying and neutering—is, of course, one solution, but it's a final one. A sterilized or castrated animal can never reproduce.

A dog and children

Dogs and children are a great combination. They can play together and get great pleasure out of each other's company. Moreover children need to learn how to handle living beings; they develop respect and a sense of responsibility by caring for a dog (or other pets). However sweet a dog is, children must understand that it is an animal and not a toy. A dog isn't

comfortable when it's messed around with. It can become frightened, timid and even aggressive. So make it clear what a dog likes and what it doesn't. Look for ways the child can play with the dog, perhaps a game of hide and seek where the child hides and the dog has to find it. Even a simple tennis ball can give enormous pleasure. Children must learn to leave a dog in peace when it doesn't want to play any more. The dog must also have its own place where it's not disturbed. Have children help with your dog's care as much as possible. A strong bond will be the result.

The arrival of a baby also means changes in the life of a dog. Before the birth you can help get the dog acquainted with the new situation. Let it sniff at the new things in the house and it will quickly accept them. When the baby has arrived involve the dog as much as possible in day-by-day events, but make sure it gets plenty of attention too. NEVER leave a dog alone with young children. Crawling infants sometimes make unexpected movements, which can easily frighten a dog. And infants are hugely curious, and may try to find out whether the tail is really fastened to the dog, or whether its eyes come out, just like they do with their cuddly toys. But a dog is a dog and it will defend itself when it feels threatened.

Where to buy

There are various ways to acquire a dog. The decision for a puppy or an adult dog will also define for the most part where to buy your dog. If it's to be a puppy, then you need to find a breeder with a litter. If you chose a popular breed like the Golden Retriever there is choice enough. But you may also face the problem that there are so many puppies on sale that have only been bred for profit's sake. You can see how many puppies are for sale by looking in the newspaper. Some of these dogs have a pedigree, but many don't. Breeders often don't watch out for breed-specific illnesses and in-breeding; puppies are separated from their mother as fast as possible and are thus insufficiently socialized. Never buy a puppy that is too young, or whose mother you weren't able to see.

Fortunately there are also enough bona-fide breeders of Golden Retrievers. Try to visit a number of breeders before you actually buy your puppy. Ask if the breeder is prepared to help you after you've bought your puppy and to help you find solutions for any problems that may come up.

A breeder that feels responsible for his breed will never mate parent dogs suffering from a congenital condition. Breeders that are members of the breed association are expelled if they do

use such animals. But there are plenty of breeders that are not association members. They don't have to keep to the breeding regulations and, in principle, can also breed with unhealthy animals. A reliable breeder can also face problems with congenital conditions within his population, of course, but if he works according to the breed association guidelines, this risk is reduced. Especially when buying such a popular dog as the Golden Retriever, it can not be overstated how extremely important it is to contact (via the breed association) a good, reliable breeder!

Finally, you must realize that a pedigree is nothing more or less than a proof of descent. The kennel club also issues pedigrees to the young of parents that suffer from a congenital condition, or that have never been checked for them. A pedigree says nothing about the health of the parent dogs or of your puppy.

If you're looking for an adult dog, it's best to contact the breed association, who often help place adult dogs that can no longer be kept by their owners because of personal circumstances (impulse buying, moving, divorce, etc.).

Things to watch out for

Buying a puppy is no simple matter. You must pay attention to the following:

- Never buy a puppy on impulse, even if it is love at first sight. A dog is a living being that will need care and attention over a long period. It is not a toy that you can put away when you're

Ten golden puppy rules

1. Walk your puppy in doses followed by one hour play, a feed and then three hours sleep.
2. Don't let your puppy run endlessly after a ball or stick.
3. Don't let your puppy romp wildly with large, heavy dogs.
4. Never let your puppy play on a full tummy.
5. Don't give your puppy anything to drink straight after a meal.
6. Don't let your puppy run up and down steps for the first year. Be careful with shiny floors.
7. Don't add supplements to ready-made food.
8. Watch out for your puppy's weight. Being overweight can contribute to bone abnormalities.
9. Give your puppy a quiet place to sleep.
10. Pick your puppy up carefully, one hand under its chest, the other under its hindquarters.

done with it.

- Take a good look at the mother. Is she calm, nervous, aggressive, well cared-for or neglected? The behavior and condition of the mother is not only a sign of the quality of the breeder, but also of the puppy you're about to buy.
- Avoid buying a puppy whose mother has been kept only in a kennel. A young dog needs as many different impressions as possible in its first few months, including living in a family group. It gets used to people and possibly other pets. Kennel dogs miss these experiences and are inadequately socialized.
- The mother should not have had more than five litters. Check this with the breeder or the breed association (you can find the address at the back of this book).
- Always ask to see the parents' papers (vaccination certificates, pedigrees). Both parents should have been X-rayed for potential hip dysplasia, and they should have an official certificate to prove it. They should also have certificates for an eye examination, which must not be older than one year (see the chapter Your Golden Retriever's health).
- Never buy a puppy younger than eight weeks.
- Put all agreements with the breeder in writing. A model agreement is available from the breed association.

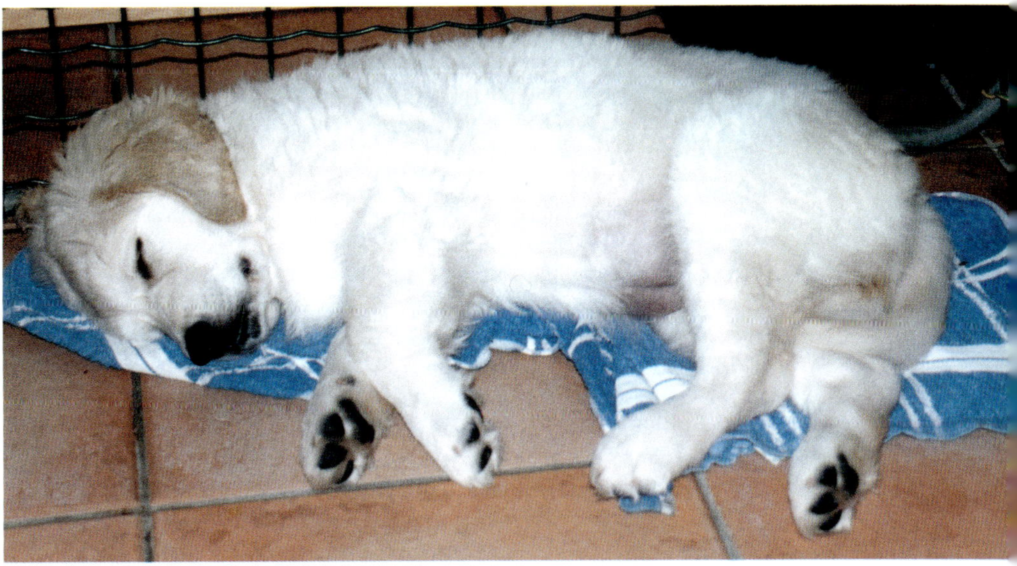

Traveling with your Golden Retriever

There are a few things to think about before traveling with your dog. While one dog may enjoy traveling, another may hate it.

You may like vacations in far-away places, but it's questionable whether your dog will enjoy them as much.

That very first trip

The first trip of a puppy's life is also the most nerve-wracking. This is the trip from the breeder's to its new home. If possible, pick up your puppy in the morning. It then has the whole day to get used to the new situation. Ask the breeder not to feed it that day. The young animal will be overwhelmed by all kinds of new experiences. Firstly, it's away from its mother; it's in a small room (the car) with all its different smells, noises and strange people. So there's a big chance that the puppy will be car-sick this first time, with the annoying consequence that it will remember riding in the car as an unpleasant experience.

So it's important to make this first trip as pleasant as possible. When picking up a puppy, always take someone with you who can sit in the back seat with the puppy on his or her lap and talk to it calmly. If it's too warm for the puppy, a place on the floor at the feet of your companion is ideal. The pup will lie there relatively quietly and may even take a nap. Ask the breeder for a cloth or something else from its nest that carries a familiar scent. The puppy can lie on this in the car, and it will also help if it feels alone during the first nights at home.

If the trip home is a long one, then stop for a break (once in a while). Let your puppy roam and sniff around (on the leash!), have a little drink and, if necessary, do its business. Do take care to lay an old towel in the car. It can happen that the puppy, in its nervousness, may urinate or be sick. It's also good advice to give a puppy positive experiences with car journeys. Make short trips to nice places where you can walk and play with it. It can be a real nuisance if your dog doesn't like riding in a car. After all, once in a while you will have to take it to certain places, such as the veterinarian or to visit friends and acquaintances.

Taking your Golden Retriever on vacation

When making vacation plans, you also need to think about what you're going to do with your dog during that time. Are you taking it with you, putting it into a vacation kennel or leaving it with friends? In any event there are a number of things you need to do in good time. If you want to take your dog with you, you need to be sure in advance that it will be welcome at your vacation home and what the rules there are. If you're going abroad it will need certain vaccinations and a health certificate, which normally need to be done four weeks before departure. Your veterinarian can give you the most recent information.

If your trip is to a tick-infested area, ask for a treatment against ticks (you can read more about

this in the *Parasites* chapter). Although dog-owners usually enjoy taking their dog on vacation, you must seriously ask yourself whether the dog feels that way too. Goldens certainly don't always feel comfortable in a hot climate. Days spent riding in a car are also often not their preference, and some dogs suffer badly from car-sickness. There are good medicines for this, but it's questionable whether you're doing your dog a favor with them. If you do decide to take it with you, make regular stops at safe places during your journey, so that your dog can have a good run. Take plenty of fresh drinking water with you, as well as the food your dog is used to.

Don't leave your dog in the car standing in the sun. It can quickly be overcome by the heat, with even fatal consequences. If you have to leave your dog in the car, park the car in the shade if at all possible, and leave a window open for a little fresh air. Even if you've taken these precautions, never stay away long!

If you're traveling by plane or ship, make sure that your dog can travel with you and that you know what rules you need to observe. You will need some time to make all the arrangements. Maybe you decide not to take your dog with you, and you then need to find somewhere for it to stay. Arrangements for a place in a vacation kennel need to be made well in advance, and there may be certain vaccinations required, which need to be given a minimum of one month before the stay.

If your dog can't be accommodated in the homes of relatives or friends, it might be possible to have an acquaintance stay in your house. This also needs to be arranged well in advance, as it may be difficult to find someone that can do this.

Always ensure that your dog can be traced should it run away or get lost while on vacation. A tag with home and vacation address attached to your dog's collar can avoid a lot of problems.

Moving

Dogs generally become more attached to humans than to the house they live in. Changing residences is usually not a problem for them. But it can be useful before moving to let the dog get to know its new home and the area around it. If you can, leave your dog with relatives or friends (or in a kennel) on the day of the move. The chance of it running away or getting lost is then reduced. When your move is complete, you can pick up your dog and let it quietly get familiar with its new home and environment. Give it its own place in the house at once and it will quickly adapt. During the first week or so, always walk your dog on a leash because an animal can also get lost in new surroundings. Always take a different route so it quickly gets to know the neighborhood.

Don't forget to get your new address and phone number engraved on the dog's tag. Send a change of address notice to the institution that has any chip or tattoo data. Dogs must sometimes be registered in a new community, and you must pay for a dog license.

Nutrition and feeding your Golden Retriever

A dog will actually eat a lot more than just meat.

In the wild it would eat its prey complete with skin and fur, including the bones, stomach, and the innards with their semi-digested vegetable material. In this way the dog supplements its meat menu with the vitamins and minerals it needs. This is also the basis for feeding a domestic dog.

Ready-made foods

It's not easy for a layman to put together a complete menu for a dog, with all the necessary proteins, fats, vitamins and minerals in just the right proportions and quantities. Meat alone is certainly not a complete meal for a dog. It contains too little calcium. A calcium deficiency over time will lead to bone defects, and for a fast-growing puppy this can lead to serious skeleton deformities.

If you put its food together yourself, you can easily give your dog too much in terms of vitamins and minerals, which can also be bad for your dog's health. You can avoid these problems by giving it ready-made food of a good brand. These products are well-balanced and contain everything your dog needs. Supplements such as vitamin preparations are superfluous. The amount of food your dog needs depends on its weight and activity level. You can find guidelines on the packaging. Split the food into two meals per day if possible, and always ensure there's a dish of fresh drinking water next to its food.

Give your dog time to digest its food, don't let it outside immediately after a meal. A dog should also never play on a full stomach. This can cause stomach torsion (the stomach turning over), which can be fatal for your dog.

Because the food needs of a dog depend, among other things, on its age and way of life, there are many different types of dog food available. There are "light" foods for less active dogs, "energy" foods for working dogs and "senior" foods for the older dog. There are also special foods for large breed puppies like Goldens. Consult your veterinarian for advice on the proper diet.

Canned and dry foods

Ready-made foods available at pet stores or in the supermarket can roughly be split into canned and dry food. Whichever form you choose, ensure that it's a complete food with all the necessary substances. You can see this on the packaging.

Most dogs love canned food. Although the better brands are composed well, they do have one disadvantage: they are soft. A dog fed only on canned food will sooner or later have problems with its teeth (plaque, tartar, and periodontal disease). Besides canned food, give your dog hard foods at certain times or a dog chew.

The advantage of dry foods is that they are hard, forcing the dog to use its jaws, removing plaque and massaging the gums.

Dog chew products

Naturally, once in a while you want to spoil your dog with something extra. Don't give it pieces of cheese or sausage as these contain too much salt and fat. There are various products available that a dog will find delicious and which are also healthy, especially for its teeth. You'll find a large range of varying quality in the pet store.

The butcher's left-overs

The bones of slaughtered animals have traditionally been given to the dog, and dogs are crazy about them, but they are not without risks. Pork and poultry bones can splinter and cause serious injury to the intestines. Beef bones are more suitable, but they must first be cooked to kill off dangerous bacteria. Pet stores carry a range of smoked, cooked and beef and pork products such as pig ears and cow hooves. Feed these in moderation; some animals do not tolerate them well.

Fresh meat

If you do want to give your dog fresh meat occasionally, never give it raw, but always boiled or roasted. Raw (or not fully cooked) beef, pork, or chicken can contain life-threatening bacteria.

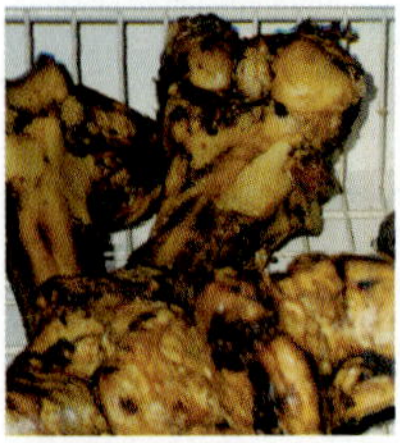

Beef bones

Rawhide chews

Dog chews are mostly made of beef or buffalo hide. Chews are usually knotted or pressed hide. Other than these forms, a dog can enjoy little shoes, twisted sticks, balls and various other shapes; nice to look at and a nice change. Use rawhide chews in moderation; some dogs' digestive systems do not tolerate them.

Munchy sticks

Munchy sticks are green, yellow, red or brown colored sticks of various thickness. They consist of ground buffalo hide with a number of often-undefined additives. The composition and quality of these between-meal treats is not always clear. Some are fine, but there have also been sticks found to contain high levels of cardboard and even paint residues. Choose a product whose ingredients are clearly described.

Overweight?

Recent investigations have shown that many dogs are overweight. A dog usually gets fat because of over-feeding and lack of exercise. Use of medicines or a disease is rarely the cause. Dogs that get fat are often given too much food or treats between meals. Gluttony or boredom can also be a cause, and a dog often puts on weight

You'll find a large range of dog chew products in the pet store.

following spaying or castration. Due to changes in hormone levels it becomes less active and consumes less energy. Finally, simply too little exercise alone can lead to a dog becoming overweight.

You can use the following rule of thumb to check whether your dog is overweight: you should be able to feel its ribs, but not see them. If you can't feel its ribs then your dog is fat. Overweight dogs live a passive life, they play too little and tire quickly. They also suffer from all kinds of medical problems (problems in joints and heart conditions). They usually die younger too.

So it's important to make sure your dog doesn't get fat. Always follow the guidelines on food packaging. Adapt them if your dog is less active or gets lots of snacks. Try to make sure your dog gets plenty of exercise by playing and running with it as much as you can. If your dog starts to show signs of putting on weight you can switch to a low-calorie food. If it's really fat and reducing its food quantity doesn't help, then a special diet is the only solution.

Rawhide chews

Munchy sticks

Caring for your Golden Retriever

Good (daily) care is extremely important for your dog. A well-cared for dog is less likely to get sick.

Caring for your dog is not only necessary, but is also a pleasure. Master and dog are giving each other some attention, and it's an excellent opportunity for a game and a hug.

The coat

Caring for your dog's coat involves regular brushing and combing, together with checking for parasites such as fleas. How often a dog needs to be brushed and combed depends on the length of its coat. Brush your Golden Retriever once a week. If it's shedding, then it needs brushing every day to avoid tangles in its coat. Use the right equipment for taking care of the coat. Combs should not be too sharp and you should use a rubber or natural hairbrush. Always comb from the head back towards the tail, following the direction of the hair.

If you get a puppy used to being brushed from an early age, it will enjoy having its coat cared for. Only bathe a dog when it's really necessary, usually once every four weeks to avoid stripping the coat of natural protective oils. Always use a special dog shampoo and make sure it doesn't get into the dog's eyes or ears. Rinse the suds out thoroughly. A veterinarian can prescribe special medicinal shampoos for some skin conditions. Always follow the instructions to the letter.

Good flea prevention is highly important to avoid skin and coat problems. Fleas must be treated not only on the dog itself but also in its surroundings (see the chapter *Parasites*).

Coat problems can also occur due to an allergy to certain food substances. In such cases, a veterinarian can prescribe a hypo-allergenic diet.

Teeth

A dog must be able to eat properly to stay in good condition, so it needs healthy teeth. Check its teeth regularly. Get in touch with your veterinarian if you suspect that all is not well. A regular diet of hard, dry food can help keep your dogs teeth clean and healthy. There are special dog chews on the market that help prevent plaque and help keep the animal's breath fresh.

What really helps is regular tooth brushing. You can use special toothbrushes for dogs, but a finger wrapped in a small piece of gauze will also do the job.

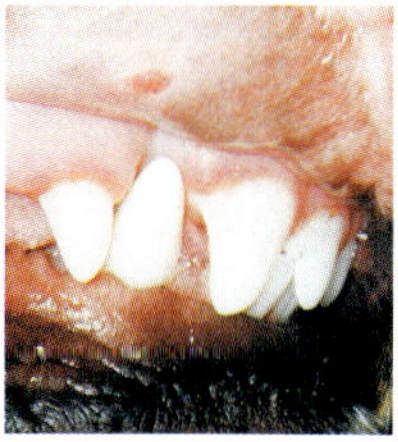

Get your dog used to having its teeth cleaned at an early age and you won't have problems. Never use human toothpaste. Your veterinarian or pet store can provide you with toothpaste formulated especially for dogs.

You can even teach an older dog to have its teeth cleaned. With a dog chew as a reward it will certainly be happy.

Nails

On a dog that regularly walks on hard surfaces, its nails usually grind themselves down. In this case there's no need to clip their nails. But it wouldn't do any harm to check their length now and again, especially on dogs that don't get out on the streets often. Using a piece of paper, you can easily see whether its nails are too long. If you can push the paper between the nail and the ground when the dog is standing, then the nail is the right length.

Nails that are too long can bother a dog. It can injure itself when scratching, so they must be kept trimmed. You can buy special nail clippers in pet stores. Be careful not to clip back too far as you could damage the cuticle, which can bleed profusely. If you feel unsure, have this necessary task done by a veterinarian or a pet groomer.

Eyes

A dog's eyes should be cleaned daily. Mucus discharge from sleep and little lumps of dried eye moisture can get into the corners of the eye. You can easily remove them by wiping them downward with your thumb. If you don't like doing that, use a piece of tissue or toilet paper.

Keeping your dog's eyes clean will take only a few seconds a day, so do it every day. If the discharge becomes yellow and slimy, this points to heavy irritation or an infection. Seek veterinary care for this condition. Conditions on the "third eye-lid" must be corrected surgically.

Ears

The ears are often forgotten when caring for dogs, but they must be checked at least once a week. If its ears are very dirty or have too much wax, you must clean them. This should preferably be done with a clean cotton cloth, moistened with lukewarm water. NEVER enter the ear canal with any object. If you do neglect cleaning your dog's ears there's a substantial risk of infection. A dog that is constantly scratching at its ears might be suffering from dirty ears, an ear infection or ear mites, making a visit to the veterinarian essential.

Raising your Golden Retriever

It is very important that your dog is properly raised and is obedient. Not only will this bring you more pleasure, but it's also nicer for your environment.

This also applies to the Golden Retriever, despite the fact that it is well known for its pleasant and problem-free character.

A puppy can learn what he may and may not do by playing. Rewards and consistency are important tools in bringing up a dog. Reward it with your voice, a stroke or something tasty and it will quickly learn to obey. A puppy-training course can also help you along the way.

(Dis)obedience

A dog that won't obey you is not just a problem for you, but also for your surroundings. It's therefore important to avoid unwanted behavior. In fact, this is what training your dog is all about, so get started early. "Start 'em young!" applies to dogs too. An untrained dog is not just a nuisance, but can also cause dangerous situations, including running into the road, chasing joggers or jumping at people. A dog must be trained out of this undesirable behavior as quickly as possible. The longer you let it go on, the more difficult it will become to correct. The best thing to do is to attend a special obedience course. This won't only help to correct the dog's behavior, but its owner also learns how to handle undesirable behavior at home. A dog must not only obey its master during training, but at home too.

Always be consistent when training good behavior and correcting annoying behavior. This means a dog may always behave in a certain way, or must never behave that way. Reward it for good behavior and never punish it after the fact for any wrongdoing. If your dog finally comes after you've been calling it a long time, then reward it. If you're angry because you had to wait so long, it may feel it's actually being punished for coming. It will probably not obey at all the next time for fear of punishment.

Try to take no notice of undesirable behavior. Your dog will perceive your reaction (even a negative one) as a reward for this behavior. If you need to correct the dog, then do this immediately. Use your voice or grip it by the scruff of its neck and push it to the ground. This is the way a mother dog calls her pups to order. Rewards for good behavior are, by far, preferable to punishment; they always get a better result.

Housetraining

The very first training (and one of the most important) that a dog needs is housetraining or housebreaking. The basis for good housetraining is keeping a good eye on your puppy. If you pay attention, you will notice that it will sniff a long time and do turns around a certain spot before doing its business there. Pick it up gently and place it outside, always at the same place. Reward it abundantly if it does its business there. Another good moment for housetraining is after eating or sleeping. A puppy often needs to do its business at these times. Let it relieve itself before playing with it, otherwise it will forget to do so and you'll not reach your goal.

For the first few days, take your puppy out for a walk just after it's eaten or woken up. It will quickly learn the meaning, especially if it's rewarded with a dog biscuit for a successful attempt. Of course, it's not always possible to go out after every snack or snooze. Lay newspapers at different spots in the house. Whenever the pup needs to do its business, place it on a newspaper. After some time it will start to look for a place itself. Then start to reduce the number of newspapers until there is just one left, at the front or back door. The puppy will learn to go to the door if it needs to relieve itself. Then you put it on the leash and go out with it. Finally you can remove

the last newspaper. Your puppy is now house-trained. One thing that certainly won't work is punishing an accident after the fact. A dog whose nose is rubbed in its urine or its droppings won't understand that at all. It will only get frightened of you. Rewarding works much better than punishment. An indoor kennel or crate can be a good tool to help in house-training. A puppy won't foul its own sleeping area, so a crate can be a good solution for the night, or during periods in the day when you can't watch it. But a crate must not become a prison where your dog is locked up day and night.

First exercises

The basic commands for an obedient dog are those for sit, lie down, come and stay. But a puppy should first learn its name. Use it as much as possible from the first day on followed by a friendly "Come!" Reward it with your voice and a stroke when it comes to you. Your puppy will quickly recognize the intention and has now learned its first command in a playful manner. Don't appear too strict towards a young puppy, and don't always punish it immediately if it doesn't always react in the right way. When you call your puppy to you in this way have it come right to you. You can teach a pup to sit by holding a piece of dog biscuit above his nose and then slowly moving it backwards. The puppy's head will also move backwards until its hind legs slowly go down. At that moment you call "Sit!" After a few attempts, it will quickly know this nice game. Use the "Sit!" command before you give your dog its food, put it on the leash, or before it's allowed to cross the street.

Teaching the command to lie down is similar. Instead of moving the piece of dog biscuit backwards, move it down vertically until your hand reaches the ground and then forwards. The dog will also move its forepaws forwards and lie down on its own. At that moment call "Lie down!" or "Lay!" This command is useful when you want a dog to be quiet.

Two people are needed for the "Come!" command. One holds the dog back while the other runs away. After about fifteen yards, he stops and enthusiastically calls "Come!" The other person now lets the dog free, and it should obey the command at once. Again you reward it abundantly. The "Come!" command is useful in many situations and good for safety, too.

A dog learns to stay from the sitting or lying position. While its sitting or lying down, you call the command: "Stay!" and then step back one step. If the dog moves with you, quietly put it back in position, without displaying anger.

If you do react angrily, you're actually punishing it for coming to you, and you'll only confuse your dog. It can't understand that coming is rewarded one time, and punished another. Once the dog stays nicely reward it abundantly. Practice this exercise with increasing distances (at first no more than three feet). The "Stay!" command is useful when getting out of the car.

Courses

Obedience courses to help you bring up your dog are available across the country. These courses are not just informative, but also fun for dog and master.

With a puppy, you can begin with a puppy course. This is designed to provide the basic training. A puppy that has attended such a course has learned about all kinds of things that will confront it in later life: other dogs, humans, traffic and what these mean. The puppy will also learn obedience and to follow a number of basic commands. Apart from all that, attention will be given to important subjects such as brushing, being alone, riding in a car, and doing its business in the right places.

The next step after a puppy course is a course for young dogs. This course repeats the basic exercises

and ensures that the growing dog doesn't get into bad habits. After this, the dog can move on to an obedience course for full-grown dogs. For more information on where to find courses in your area, contact your local kennel club. You can get its address from the American Kennel Club.

Play and toys

There are various ways to play with your dog. You can romp and run with it, but also play a number of games, such as retrieving, tug-of-war, hide-and-seek and catch. A tennis ball is ideal for retrieving, you can play tug-of-war with an old sock or a special tugging rope. Start with tug-of-war only when your dog is a year old. A puppy must first get its second teeth and then they need several months to strengthen. There's a real chance of your dog's teeth becoming deformed if you start too young. You can use almost anything for a game of hide-and-seek. A frisbee is ideal for catching games. Never use too small a ball for games. It can easily get lodged in the dog's throat.

Play is extremely important. Not only does it strengthen the bond between dog and master, but it's also healthy for both. Make sure that you're the one that ends the game. Only stop when the dog has brought back the ball or frisbee, and make sure you always win the tug-of-war. This confirms your dominant position in the hierarchy. Use these toys only during play so that the dog doesn't forget their significance. When choosing a special dog toy, remember that dogs are hardly careful with them. So always buy toys of good quality that a dog can't easily destroy.

Be very careful with small branches and twigs. The latter, particularly, can easily splinter. A splinter of wood in your dog's throat or intestines can cause awful problems. Throwing small branches or twigs can also be dangerous. If they stick into the ground a dog can easily run into them with an open mouth.

If you would like to do more than just play games, you can now also play sports with your dog. For people who want to do more, there are various other sporting alternatives such as Agility and Obedience.

Aggressiveness

Golden Retrievers are practically never aggressive. But even they can sometimes be difficult with other animals or people, so it's good to understand more about the background of aggression in dogs.

There are two types of aggressive behavior in dogs: anxious-aggressive and dominant-aggressive. An anxious-aggressive dog can be recognized by its pulled back ears and its low position. It will have pulled in its lips, showing its teeth. This dog is aggressive because it's very frightened and feels cornered. It would prefer to run away, but if it can't then it will bite to defend itself. It will grab its victim anywhere it can. The attack is usually brief and, as soon as the dog can see a way to escape, it's gone. In a confrontation with other dogs, it will normally turn out as the loser. It can become even more aggressive once it's realized that people or other dogs are afraid of it. This behavior cannot be corrected just like that. First you have to try and understand what the dog is afraid of. Professional advice is a good idea here because the wrong approach can easily make the problem worse.

The dominant-aggressive dog's body talk is different. Its ears stand up and its tail is raised and stiff. This dog will always go for its victim's arms, legs or throat. It is extremely self-assured and highly placed in the dog hierarchy. Its attack is a display of power rather than a consequence of fear. This dog needs to know who's boss. You must bring it up rigorously and with a strong hand. An obedience course can help.

A dog may also bite itself because it's in pain. This is a natural defensive reaction. In this case try to resolve the dog's fear as far as possible. Reward him for letting you get to the painful spot. Be careful, because a dog in pain may also bite its master! Muzzling it can help prevent problems if you have to do something that may be painful. Never punish a dog for this type of aggression!

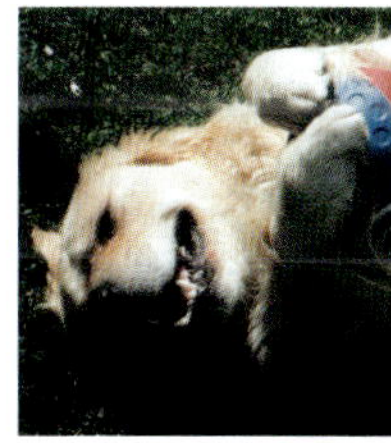

Fear

The source of anxious behavior can often be traced to the first weeks of a dog's life. A shortage of new experiences during this important phase (also called the "socialization phase") has great influence on its later behavior. A dog that never encountered humans, other dogs or animals during the socialization phase will be afraid of them later. This fear is common in dogs brought up in a barn or kennel, with almost no contact with humans. Fear can lead to aggressive behavior, so it's important that a puppy gets as many new impressions as possible in the first weeks of its life. Take it with you into town in the car, walk it down busy streets and allow it to have plenty of contact with people, other dogs and other animals.

It's a huge task to turn an anxious, poorly socialized dog into a real pet. It will probably take an enormous amount of attention, love, patience and energy to get such an animal used to everything around it. Reward it often and

give it plenty of time to adapt and, over time, it will learn to trust you and become less anxious.
Try not to force anything, because that will always have the reverse effect. Here too, an obedience course can help a lot. A dog can be especially afraid of strangers. Have visitors give it something tasty as a treat. Put a can of dog biscuits by the door so that your visitors can spoil your dog when they arrive. Here again, don't try to force anything. If the dog is still frightened, leave it in peace.

Dogs are often frightened in certain situations; well-known examples are thunderstorms and fireworks. In these cases try to ignore their anxious behavior. If you react to their whimpering and whining, it's the same as rewarding it. If you ignore its fear completely, the dog will quickly learn that nothing is wrong. You can speed up this "learning process" by rewarding its positive behavior.

Rewarding

Rewarding forms the basis for bringing up a dog. Rewarding good behavior works far better than punishing bad behavior and rewarding is also much more fun. Over time the opinions on

upbringing for dogs have gradually changed. In the past the proper way to correct bad behavior was a sharp pull on the leash. Today, experts view rewards as a positive incentive to get dogs to do what we expect of them. There are many ways to reward a dog. The usual ways are a stroke or a friendly word, even without a tasty treat to go with it. Of course, a piece of dog biscuit does wonders when you're training a puppy. Be sure you always have something delicious in your pocket to reward good behavior.

Another form of reward is play. Whenever a dog notices you have a ball in your pocket, it won't go far from your side. As soon as you've finished playing, put the ball away. This way your dog will always do its best in exchange for a game.

Despite the emphasis you put on rewarding good behavior, a dog can sometimes be a nuisance or disobedient. You must correct such behavior immediately. Always be consistent: once "no" must always be "no."

Barking

Dogs that bark too much and too often are a nuisance for their surroundings. A dog-owner may tolerate barking up to a point, but neighbors are often annoyed by the unnecessary noise. Don't encourage your puppy to bark and yelp. Of course, it should be able to announce its presence, but if it goes on barking it must be called to order with a strict "Quiet!" If a puppy fails to obey, just hold its muzzle closed with your hand.

A dog will sometimes bark for long periods when left alone. It feels threatened and tries to get someone's attention by barking. There are special training programs for this problem, where dogs learn that being alone is nothing to be afraid of, and that its master will always return. You can practice this with your dog at home. Leave the room and come back in at once. Reward your dog if it stays quiet. Gradually increase the length of your absences and keep rewarding it as long as it remains quiet.

Never punish the dog if it does bark or yelp. It will never understand punishment afterwards, and this will only make the problem worse. Never go back into the room as long as your dog is barking, as it will view this as a reward. You might want to make the dog feel more comfortable by switching the radio on for company during your absence. It will eventually learn that you always come back and the barking will reduce. If you don't get the required result, attend an obedience course.

Reproduction

Dogs, and thus Golden Retrievers, follow their instincts, and reproduction is one of nature's important processes.

For people who enjoy breeding dogs this is a positive circumstance. Those who simply want a "cozy companion" however, will miss the regular adventures with females on heat and unrestrainable males like a toothache. But knowing a little about reproduction in dogs will help you to understand why they behave the way they do, and what measures you need to take when this happens.

Breeding recommendations

Breeding dogs is much more than simply 1+1= many. If you're planning to breed your Golden Retriever, consult with your local kennel club for guidelines.

The kennel clubs place strict conditions on animals used for breeding. They must be examined for possible congenital defects (see the chapter *Your Golden Retriever's health*). This is the breeder's first obligation.

The female in season

Bitches become sexually mature at about eight to twelve months. Then they go into season for the first time. They are "in heat" for two to three weeks. During this period they discharge little drops of blood and they are very attractive to males. The bitch is fertile during the second half of her season, and will accept a male to mate. The best time for mating is then between the ninth and thirteenth day of her season. A female's first season is often shorter and less severe than those that follow. If you do want to breed your female you must allow this first (and sometimes the second) season to pass. Most bitches go into season twice per year. If you do plan to breed your Golden in the future, then spaying is not an option to prevent unwanted offspring.

Pseudopregnancy (false pregnancy)

A false pregnancy is a not uncommon occurrence. The female behaves as if she has a litter. She takes all kinds of things to her resting place and treats them like puppies. Her milk teats swell and sometimes milk is actually produced. The female will sometimes behave aggressively towards people or other animals, as if she is defending her young. False pregnancies usually begin two months after a season and can last a number of weeks. If it happens to a bitch once, it will often then occur after every season. If the condition repeats itself, spaying is the best solution, because continual phantom pregnancies increase the risk of womb or teat conditions.

Preparing to breed

If you do plan to breed a litter of puppies, you must first wait for your female to be physically and mentally full-grown. In any event you must let her first season pass. To mate a bitch, you need a male. You could simply let her out on the street and she will quickly return home pregnant. But if you have a pure-bred Golden Retriever, then it certainly makes sense to mate her with the best possible candidate, even if she has no

pedigree. Proceed with caution and think especially about the following: Accompanying a bitch through pregnancy, birth and the first eight to twelve weeks afterwards is a time-consuming affair. Never breed Golden Retrievers that have congenital defects, and this also applies to dogs without papers. The same goes for hyperactive, nervous and shy dogs. If your Golden Retriever does have a pedigree, then mate her with a dog that also has one. For more information, contact the breed association.

Pregnancy

It's often difficult to tell at first when a bitch is pregnant. Only after about four weeks can you feel the pups in her belly. She will now slowly get fatter and her behavior will usually change. Her teats will swell during the last few weeks of pregnancy. The average pregnancy lasts 63 days and costs her a lot of energy. In the beginning she is fed her normal amount of food, but her nutritional needs increase dramatically during the second half of the pregnancy. Give her approximately fifteen percent more food each week from the fifth week on. The mother-to-be needs extra energy and proteins during this phase of her pregnancy. During the last weeks you can give her a concentrated food, rich in energy, such as dry puppy food. Divide this into several small portions per day, because she can no longer deal with large portions of food. Towards the end of the pregnancy, her energy needs can easily be one-and-a-half times more than usual.

After about seven weeks the mother will start to demonstrate nesting behavior and starts to look for a place to give birth to her young. This might be her own crate or a special birthing box. This must be ready at least a week before the birth to give the mother time to get used to it. The basket or box should preferably be in a quiet place.

The birth

The average litter is between three and nine puppies. The birth usually passes without problems. Of course, you must contact your veterinarian immediately if you suspect a problem! If you are unfamiliar with the normal birthing process, it is a good idea to discuss it with your veterinarian prior to the onset of labor.

Suckling

After birth, the mother starts to produce milk. The suckling period is very demanding. During the first three to four weeks the pups rely entirely on their mother's milk. During this time she needs extra food and fluids. This can be up to three or four times the normal amount. If she's producing too little milk, you can supplement

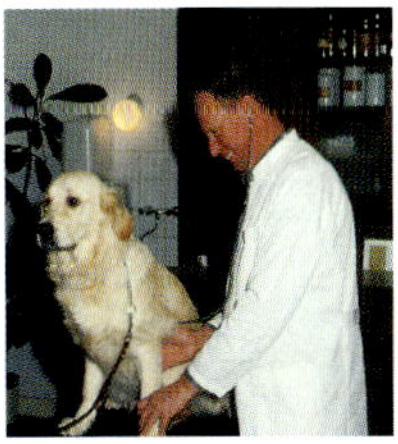

24 days after mating your veterinarian can establish whether your bitch is pregnant

the puppies with a milk-replacer. A veterinarian should be consulted if inadequate milk production is suspected.

You can give the puppies some supplemental solid food when they are three to four weeks old. There are special puppy foods available that follow on well from the mother's milk and can easily be eaten with their milk teeth.

Ideally, the puppies are fully weaned—no longer drinking their mother's milk—at an age of six or seven weeks. The mother's milk production gradually stops and her food needs also drop. Within a couple of weeks after weaning, the mother should again be getting the same amount of food as before the pregnancy.

Spaying and castration

If you do not plan to use your dog for breeding, neutering is recommended because of health benefits, population control, and the reduction of behavioral problems.

A female dog is spayed, and during this operation the uterus and the ovaries are removed. The bitch no longer goes into season and can never become pregnant. The best age for spaying is approximately six months of age, prior to the first heat cycle.

A male dog is castrated, and during this operation the testicles are removed. The best age for castration is 4-6 months.

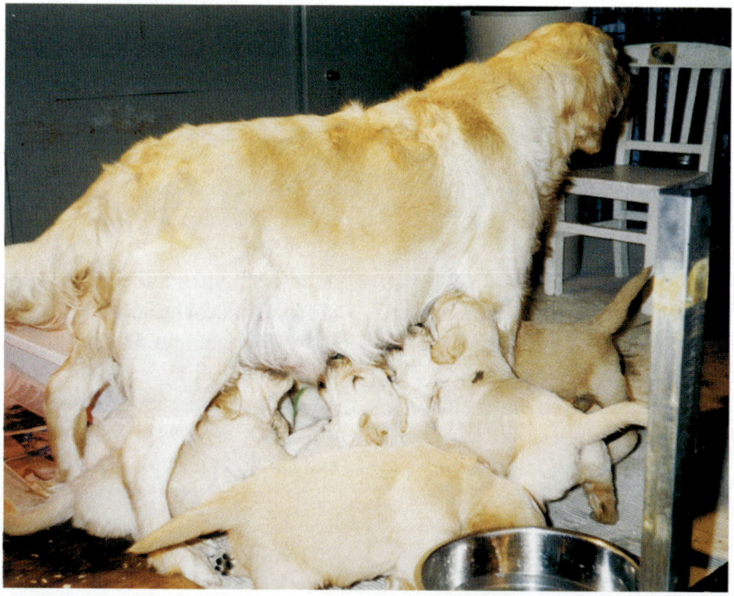

Sport and shows

The Golden Retriever is a dog that likes to be busy, especially if it can do things together with its boss.

If you regularly take part in activities with your Golden, you will not only notice that the bond between you both gets stronger, but also that your dog is quieter and more obedient.In this chapter, we'll give you a brief overview of some of the alternatives. You can get more information from the breed association.

Agility

Agility is a form of dog sport where the dog accompanied by its master has to cover a set course, getting past several obstacles on the way.
The trick is to get through as fast as possible with as few penalty points as possible. Many local dog clubs organize agility competitions.

Behavior and obedience

You can pick from a whole range of obedience training courses, beginning with a puppy course. Golden Retrievers usually enjoy this type of course. Their strong will to please means they want to perform the exercises as well as possible. After elementary obedience courses, you can train your dog for various behavior and obedience diplomas.

Rescue work

The Golden Retriever is a very capable rescue dog, but they do need thorough training first. There are groups of dog lovers that practice rescue work with their dogs as a hobby.

They follow special courses and are sometimes used in disaster situations. Contact your local breed association can give you more information.

Hunting

Hunting associations often organize hunting courses which are open to any hunting dog. A number of trainers specialize in training Golden Retrievers. Contact your local breed association.

Competitive events

The following information is courtesy the American Kennel Club Dog Care and Training:

The American Kennel Club competitive events fall into six categories: dog shows, obedience trials, tracking tests, field trials, hunting trials, and herding.

Dog shows emphasize conformation, using the breed standard to compare one dog to another. Obedience trials test how well a dog can perform a series of prescribed exercises.
Obedience is a competition of both handlers and dogs, and conformation has no bearing on the dog's ability to compete in obedience. Tracking tests require a dog to follow a trail by scent. Field trials are practical demonstrations of the dog's ability to perform. Hunting trials allow owners to receive evaluations of their dogs' hunting ability. Herding competitions involve leading a small group of livestock through a simple course.

The American Kennel Club competitive events fall into six categories: dog shows, obedience trials, tracking tests, field trials, hunting trials, and herding.

Parasites

All dogs are vulnerable to various sorts of parasite. Parasites are tiny creatures that live at the expense of another animal. They feed on blood, skin and other body substances.

There are two main types. Internal parasites live within their host animal's body (tapeworm and roundworm) and external parasites live on the animals exterior, usually in its coat (fleas and ticks), but also in its ears (ear mites).

Fleas

Fleas feed on a dog's blood. They cause not only itching and skin problems, but can also carry infections such as tapeworm. In large numbers they can cause anemia and dogs can also become allergic to a flea's saliva, which can cause serious skin conditions. So it's important to treat dog for fleas as effectively as possible, not just on the dog itself but also in its surroundings. For treatment on the animal, there are various medicines: drops for the neck and to put it in its food, flea collars, long-life sprays and flea powders. There are various sprays in pet stores that can be used to eradicate fleas in the dog's immediate surroundings. Choose a spray that kills both adult fleas and their larvae. If your dog rides in your car, you should spray that too.

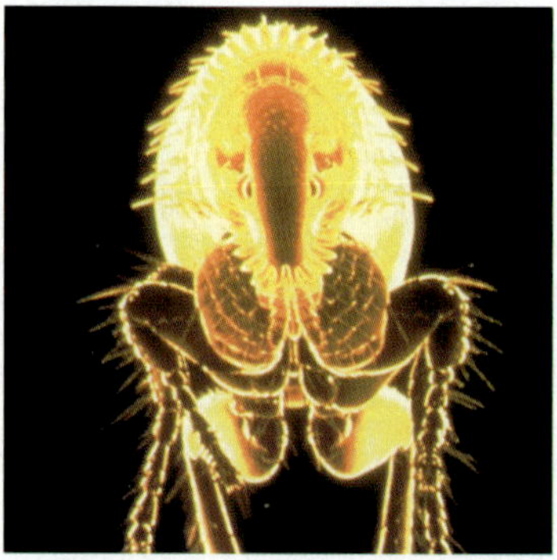

Flea

Fleas can also affect other pets, so you should treat those too. When spraying a room, cover any aquarium or fishbowl. If the spray reaches the water, it can be fatal for your fish!

Your veterinarian and pet store have a wide range of flea treatments and can advise you on the subject.

Ticks

Ticks are small, spider like parasites. They feed on the blood of the animal or person they've settled on. A tick looks like a tiny, gray-colored leather bag with eight feet. When it has sucked itself full, it can easily be five to ten times its own size and is darker in color. Dogs usually fall victim to ticks in bushes, woods or long grass. Ticks cause not only irritation by their blood sucking but can also carry a number of serious diseases. Your veterinarian can prescribe a special preventative treatment if you live or are planning to take your dog to an infested region. It is important to fight ticks as effectively as possible. Check your dog regularly, especially when its been running free in woods and bushes.

Removing a tick is simple using a tweezer. Wear gloves and grip the tick with the tweezer, as close to the dog's skin as possible and carefully pull it out. Be sure the entire tick has been removed, especially the head which has attached to the dog's skin. Wash hands thoroughly after removing ticks. You must disinfect the spot where the tick had been using iodine to prevent infection. Never soak the tick in alcohol, ether or oil. In a shock reaction the tick may discharge the infected contents of its stomach into the dog's skin.

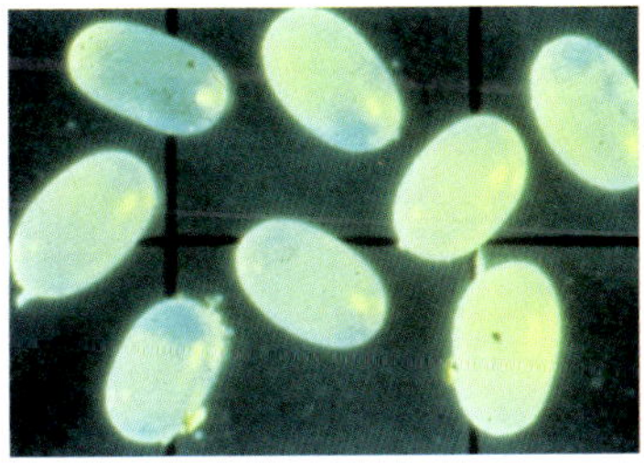

Eggs of a flea

Intestinal worms

Dogs can suffer from various types of intestinal worms, most commonly tapeworms and roundworms. Tapeworms can cause diarrhea and poor condition. With a tapeworm infection you can sometimes find small pieces of the worm (which look like grains of white rice) around the dog's anus or on its bed. In this case, the dog must be wormed. You should also check your dog for fleas, which carry the tapeworm infection.

Roundworm infection is a condition that can recur regularly. Puppies are often infected by their mother at or before birth.

Roundworms cause problems (particularly in younger dogs), such as diarrhea, loss of weight and stagnated growth. In serious cases the pup becomes thin, but with a swollen belly. It may vomit and you can then see the worms in its vomit.

The worms, resembling spaghetti, may also appear in the feces. Puppies are checked for worms and given worming medications routinely as a part of regular veterinary care. Adult dogs should be tested for worms annually and treated as recommended by your veterinarian.

Heartworms

Heartworms are parasites spread by mosquitoes. Heartworm disease can be found in almost all parts of the U.S. with greater incidence in areas with heavy mosquito populations.

The adult heartworm lives in the heart and surrounding vessels of the dog and produces offspring, called microfilaria, which circulate in the blood of the infected animal. When a mosquito bites an infected pet, the microfilaria enter the mosquito and become infective larvae. They can then infect another pet bitten by that mosquito and grow into adult heartworms, resulting in heartworm disease.

Puppies are started on a preventative medication at the first visit to the veterinarian. These medications prevent the larvae from developing into adult heartworms. Annual or biannual screening tests are then recommended, even when dogs are on heartworm preventatives.

Signs of canine heartworm diseases include coughing, difficulty breathing, weight loss, poor hair coat, and fatigue. Prompt detection and early treatment of heartworm disease is important.

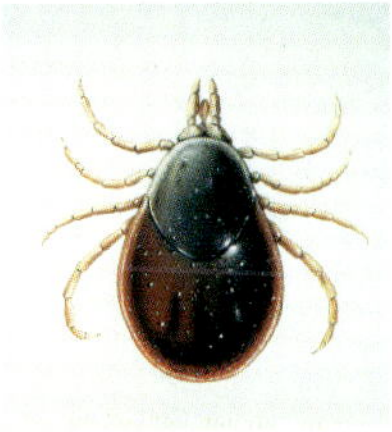

Tick

Roundworms

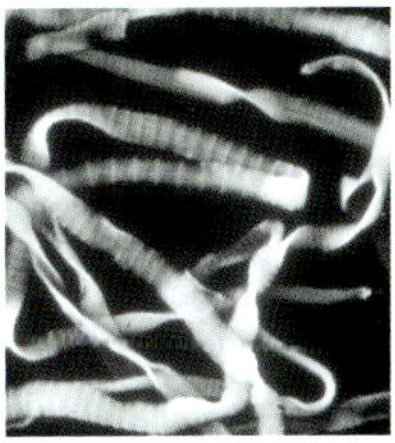

Tapeworms

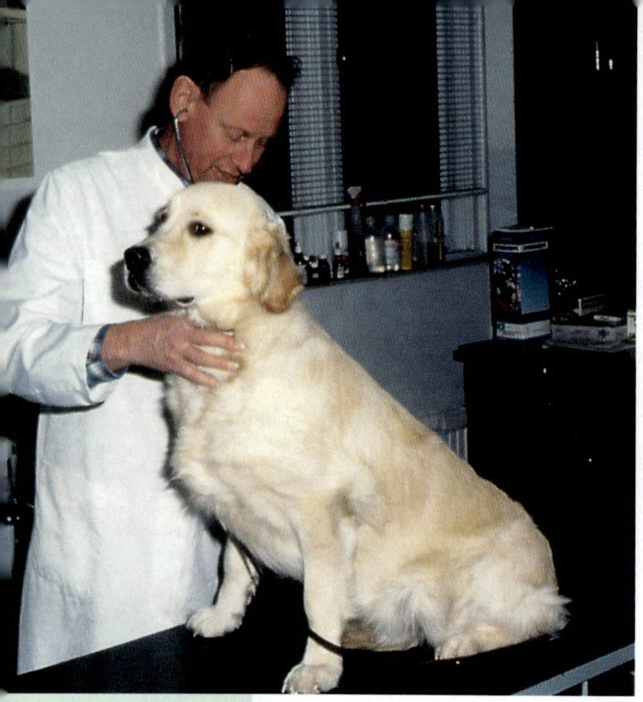

Your Golden Retriever's health

The space in this small book is too limited to go into the medical ups and downs of the Golden Retriever.

But we do want to give some brief information about ailments and disorders that affect this breed more than other dogs.

The popularity of the Golden Retriever has had its effect on the quality of the breed. For the sake of profit, a lot of breeding has taken place with unsuitable dogs, opening up more strains that are particularly vulnerable to congenital disorders.

Bone disorders

There are a number of bone disorders to which fast growing, medium to large dog breeds such as the Golden Retriever are vulnerable:

Hip Dysplasia (HD)

Many medium to large dog breeds have problems with HD, and the Golden Retriever is one of them. The breed association is hoping to keep it under control by strict examinations of parent dogs and makes these examinations mandatory for dogs to be bred.

Hip radiographs should be taken in all breeding animals by the age of two years. Animals with evidence of HD should not be used for breeding purposes.

Hip dysplasia is an abnormality of the hip joint and is characterized by varying degrees of laxity (looseness) of the hip joint. This laxity causes muscle pain due to excessive stresses on the muscles surrounding the hip joint. In many cases, HD will lead to the development of osteoarthritis at a young age. Hip dysplasia has been shown to be a polyfactorial condition, resulting from a combination of genetic, nutritional, and environmental factors. Nutrition has been shown to be a big component of the development of HD. As a result, Goldens should be fed only large breed puppy food from at least three months of age through maturity. Your veterinarian can assist you in choosing the correct diet. Because hip laxity can also occur as a traumatic event, avoid very slick surfaces and over-exertion during exercise when the puppy is young.

Veterinary care should be sought as soon as possible if your puppy shows signs of rear limb lameness.

Elbow Dysplasia (ED)
Elbow dysplasia almost always manifests itself in the first year with the development of foreleg lameness. ED is diagnosed radiographically and should be addressed as early as possible. Many cases require surgery because ED can lead to the development of early osteoarthritis. Elbow radiographs should be taken in all breeding animals, and animals with evidence of ED should not be used for breeding.

Veterinary care should be sought as early as possible if your puppy shows signs of forelimb lameness.

Osteochondrosis (OCD)
Osteochondrosis (OCD) can be a form of elbow dysplasia but is more commonly seen in the shoulder joint. Dogs show first signs of lameness at 6-8 months of age. OCD is the development of a cartilage flap within the joint

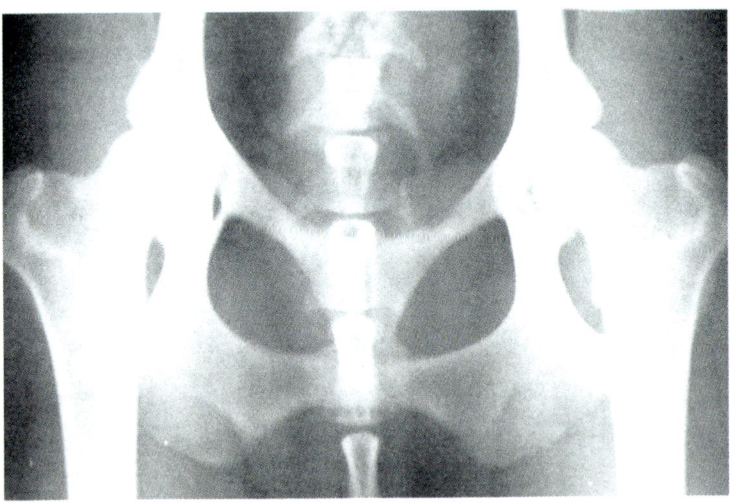

that causes progressive lameness and if not corrected surgically will result in arthritis of the shoulder. OCD is also seen less commonly in the knee and the ankle.

Eye conditions

Unfortunately, the Golden Retriever is also vulnerable to a number of eye conditions. They need to be examined for them, even if you don't plan to breed, because most of these conditions eventually lead to blindness. These are congenital conditions, so you need to be absolutely sure of the condition of the parent animals, before you buy a puppy.

Progressive Retinal Atrophy (PRA)

Up to now this condition has been more common with Labradors than with Golden Retrievers. An examination is not mandatory, but the breed association urges its member to have their dogs checked for the condition, especially if they plan to breed their dogs. Responsible breeders have their dogs examined annually. Once it's found its way into a bloodline, PRA is difficult to eradicate. The disease is a progressive degeneration of the retina that inevitably leads to blindness. In the early stages, the dog will still be able to see well in daylight until it's about five years old. But between its fifth and ninth year the dog will become totally blind.

There are two forms of PRA: the central form (day blindness or

tunnel vision) and the generalized form (night blindness).

Cataracts

Checks for cataracts are made at the same time as the checks for PRA. Cataracts cause a clouding of the lens. The condition can occur in young animals and is passed on by both parents. If only a part of the lens is affected cataracts need not lead to total blindness, but unfortunately this is the consequence in most cases

Entropion and ectropion

These are genetic conditions affecting the eyelids. With entropion the eyelids are curled inwards, with ectropion outwards. Both cause the eyelashes to lay on the cornea causing irritation, which leads to red, watering eyes. The eyes become infected and discharge pus, which can cause serious damage to the cornea and eventually even cause blindness. Entropion and ectropion can be corrected surgically.

Preventative medicine

Regular veterinary examinations are essential for the health of all puppies and adult dogs. During these visits, your veterinarian will give your pet a complete physical examination and also recommend the appropriate vaccinations, heartworm medications, and flea and tick preventions. Your veterinarian can also help with behavioral problems.

Immunization programs will vary from city to city, depending on local conditions. Your veterinarian can best recommend an appropriate vaccination schedule for puppies and adult dogs. Most puppies will receive first vaccinations at 6 weeks of age, followed by booster vaccinations every 3-4 weeks until 3-4 months of age. Adult dogs are usually vaccinated annually, depending on individual circumstances. Vaccinations will most likely include distemper, adenovirus, parvovirus, and rabies. Other vaccines administered may include hepatitis, leptospirosis, parainfluenza, corona virus, bordetella, and Lyme disease, again, according to your veterinarian's protocol.

Tips and facts

- The Golden Retriever was originally a hunting dog; it needs a rigorous upbringing!
- Get in touch with the breed association for the address of a reliable breeder.
- Don't let your puppy run endlessly after a ball or stick.
- Don't add supplements to ready-made foods.
- Don't let your puppy run up and down stairs for the first six months!
- A Golden Retriever loves to work. Do things with it.
- Never buy a Golden Retriever on impulse.
- Its first trip in a car is a real experience for a puppy; make it a pleasant one.
- Visit several breeders before you buy a puppy.
- Don't just fight the fleas, fight the larvae too.
- Don't let your dog get too fat. Not too much food and sufficient (intelligent) exercise is the rule.
- Hard food chunks and enough to chew on keep a dog's teeth healthy.
- A puppy will mean a lot of work and sometimes a few gray hairs
- Never buy a puppy if you haven't seen its mother!
- Good grooming is important for your dog's health.
- Always ask to see both parents' papers. The elbows and hips must have been X-rayed.
- Taking your dog with you on vacation? It's the best thing you can do.

Golden Retriever facts on the web

GOLDEN RETRIEVER CLUB OF AMERICA

www.grca.org

A nonprofit organization dedicated to the improvement of the breed.

AMERICAN KENNEL CLUB

www.akc.org

The official website of the American Kennel Club is a great all-around site providing everything you need to know about breeds and finding the right dog and how to raise it.

AMERICAN ANIMAL HEALTH ASSOCIATION

www.healthypet.com

The official website of the AAHA, an organization of more than 24,000 veterinary care providers committed to excellence in small animal care.

AMERICAN VETERINARY MEDICAL ASSOCIATION

www.avma.org

The official website of the national association of veterinarians that has several useful sites for dog owners regarding selection and care of dogs.

CYBERDOG

www.cyberpet.com/cyberdog

Contains down-to-earth information on dogs and dog care.

DOG NEWS

www.dognews.com

The official website of Dog News The Digest of American Dogs. An informative site containing news and information about not only purebred dogs, but all dogs.

INFODOG

www.infodog.com

A website containing listings of all the superintended dog shows in the United States and information on how to register your dog for shows.

MYPETSTOP.COM

www.mypetstop.com

A mutilingual website that offers dog care, breed and behavior information, vet advice, and breeder contacts.

WALTHAM

www.waltham.com

WALTHAM is a leading authority in pet care and this site includes extensive information on all aspects of dog care, training, and nutrition.

Breed associations

Golden Retriever Club of America
www.grca.org
The national organization for the protection and advancement of Golden Retrievers.

Master National Retriever Club
www.masternational.com
An organization that showcases the talents of retrievers.

North American Hunting Retrievers Association
www.nahra.org
A not-for-profit organization dedicated to the training and preservation of the hunting instincts of retriever breeds.